THE STORY OF ACTS

A 40-Day Guided Journey through Acts

H. HENRY WILLIAMS

FIVE OAKS CHURCH

The Story of Acts: A 40-Day Guided Journey through Acts
Copyright © 2014 H. Henry Williams
All rights reserved.

This title is also available as an ebook.
Send requests for ebook information to hwilliams87@mac.com

Requests for information should be addressed to:
Henry Williams
Five Oaks Church
4416 Radio Drive
Woodbury, MN 55129

ISBN: 1501002732
ISBN-13: 978-1501002731

Printed in the United States of America

DEDICATION

To Five Oaks Church, a church that brings
the story of God to life.

CONTENTS

ACKNOWLEDGMENTS

A special thanks goes to several of the Five Oaks Group Life writers and to my wife, Lois, for their help editing the manuscript with very short notice and significant time constraints: Mindy Wissink, Karla Pedrow, Dave Baar, and Amy Evans. Any lingering errors are purely my own.

THE STORY OF ACTS

INTRODUCTION

Imagine we are sitting across from each other in a coffee shop. Several months ago you had asked me to mentor you because I am your pastor. I agreed and set a vigorous schedule. I called it a boot camp for your spiritual life. So we met for eight weeks, five mornings a week, in this same coffee shop, and I guided you through the whole story of the Bible.

Over those eight weeks I showed you a framework for the Bible that helped you see its primary story line and how it all fits together. I gave you daily reading assignments that walked you through the Bible from beginning to end, explaining how each passage you read fit into the larger story. I filled in the gaps between the passages you did not read. The gaps were, of course, enormous, since you only read a few chapters each day, but we were able to cover most of the major players and events by the end of the eight weeks. And every day you took time to reflect on what you had read.

With this basic framework, you can now read the Bible with much better understanding and learn more from sermons and Bible studies. Additionally, what you learn sticks like never before.[1]

We had a valuable time over those forty days and decided to do something like that again. We are sitting in the coffee shop today plotting our next forty-day guided journey. This time it is through only one book of the Bible, the book of Acts.

Before we look at your reading assignment for today, there are a few things I want to tell you about the book of Acts that will help you read it with greater understanding and provide deeper value.

One Story, Second Volume

The book of Acts is actually volume two in a two-volume work. The author wrote both the Gospel of Luke and the Acts of the Apostles (these titles are not part of the original works). We know this because of the introduction to each book, the writing style, and the consistent thematic emphases.

Compare the two introductions:

> Inasmuch as many have undertaken to compile a narrative of the things that have been accomplished among us, just as those who from the beginning were eyewitnesses and ministers of the word have delivered them to us, it seemed good to me also, having followed all things closely for some time past, to write an orderly account for you, most excellent Theophilus, that you may have certainty concerning the things you have been taught. (Luke 1:1-4)

> In the first book, O Theophilus, I have dealt with all that Jesus began to do and teach. (Acts 1:1)

Early church traditions attribute these two documents to Luke, a physician and ministry companion of Paul who is mentioned in Colossians 4:14, 1 Timothy 4:11, and Philemon 24. Parts of the later chapters of Acts are even written in the first-person plural by one of Paul's traveling companions who is thought to be Luke.

We do not know the identity of Theophilus beyond these two references at the outset of both books. He is likely a Christian since Luke says he writes to confirm the truth of what Theophilus was taught about Christ. And the term "most excellent" suggests he was a person of means and influence. However, Luke may well have had a broader audience in mind, expecting his two volumes to be copied and distributed, as indeed it was.

We do not know when it was written. The most likely date is the early 60's, around the time of the events he records in Acts 28, since it is unlikely Luke would have neglected to mention Paul's death by execution in the mid-60's. Those who argue for a later date, possibly in the 70's, suggest Luke's purpose in writing was completed when Paul reached Rome at the end of Acts, therefore he had no need to go on with the story.

But here's what's most important for you to know: no serious or respected historian of this period places the date of Luke-Acts outside of the first century. Hardly any reputable scholar even places it later than the 70's! The same goes for the gospels of Matthew and Mark. John was written later, but no reputable scholar dates it later than the first century.

This means Luke-Acts was written decades (and in most cases, centuries) earlier than other gospels which were excluded from the New Testament. Some people use these gospels to question the historicity and message of Matthew, Mark, Luke, and John.

You may have heard the conspiracy theories regarding the suppression of these competing stories about Jesus on PBS, in a university classroom, or in books and movies like *The Da Vinci Code*. In every case they fail to mention how chronologically close to Christ's life and death the biblical gospels were published and how the biblical gospels clearly reflect the life and times of first-century Judaism in Palestine, as it is known through multiple ancient sources. The culture, language and philosophy reflected in these other gospels are profoundly removed from the life and times of Palestinian Judaism.

You are reading an ancient document written shortly after the events he describes took place, carefully researched and likely including material the author himself witnessed.

The Story of Acts in the Story of God
Take a look at the table of contents in your Bible. All the books that follow Acts, with the exception of 1-3 John and Revelation, were written in the time period covered by Acts. Acts and the epistles together give us a rich and textured look into the life of the early church led by the Apostles.

When we spent forty days journeying through the entire Story of God, you could not miss that the whole story is about Jesus. It points to him. This is how the New Testament writers understand the Old Testament, as is evident from the gospels and epistles. They do so because this is how Jesus read the Old Testament: "And beginning with Moses and all the Prophets, he interpreted to them in all the Scriptures the things concerning himself." (Luke 24:27; italics added)

But there is something very important that you may have missed. Jesus also taught that the entire Old Testament tells the story of Acts. Read Luke 24:44-47 carefully. Note that he reviews what he said in verse 27 to the two disciples on the road to Emmaus. Then he adds another important point:

> Then he said to them, "These are my words that I spoke to you while I was still with you, that everything written about me in the Law of Moses and the Prophets and the Psalms must be fulfilled." Then he opened their minds to understand the Scriptures, and said to them, "Thus it is written, that the Christ should suffer and on the third day rise from the dead, AND *that repentance and forgiveness of sins should be proclaimed in his name to all nations, beginning from Jerusalem.*" (Luke 24:44-47; capitalization and italics added)

Do you see it? This era he describes is what I call the "Spirit" scene in *The Story of God: A 40-Day Guided Journey through the Bible*. (See the Appendix for all ten "scenes" in the Story of God.) It is an essential part of the one story the Bible tells. The one story about Jesus doesn't end with the resurrection or ascension. The entire Old Testament also points to Jesus' continuing work through his people as they proclaim repentance and forgiveness in his name to all the nations, beginning in Jerusalem. If you look at Luke's opening words in Acts, you can see how he understood this to be so:

> In the first book, O Theophilus, I have dealt with all that Jesus *began* to do and teach. (Acts 1:1; italics added)

Luke is telling us that Acts is, by implication, the account of what Jesus continues to do and teach. However, as you read his account, it becomes evident that much of what Jesus continues to "do and teach" happens through his people, the church, and by the Holy Spirit. What the church does in the world in Jesus' name and by his power, when it reflects Jesus, is what Jesus continues to do. We are still living in this scene. Jesus continues to do and teach by the Holy Spirit through us, his people, his church.

A Table of Contents

No first-century book contained a table of contents. But authors often conceived of and presented their works in sections or "chapters" nonetheless. Luke seems to have divided Acts into six sections since he provides distinct summaries at six intervals throughout the book (Acts 6:7; 9:31; 12:24; 16:5; 19:20; 28:28-31). If we divided Luke into these six sections or chapters, it would look like this:

- Chapter 1: Acts 1:1–6:7

    And the word of God continued to increase, and the number of the disciples multiplied greatly in Jerusalem, and a great many of the priests became obedient to the faith. (Acts 6:7)

- Chapter 2: Acts 6:8–9:31

    So the church throughout all Judea and Galilee and Samaria had peace and was being built up. And walking in the fear of the Lord and in the comfort of the Holy Spirit, it multiplied. (Acts 9:31)

- Chapter 3: Acts 9:32–12:24

    But the word of God increased and multiplied. (Acts

12:24)

- Chapter 4: Acts 12:25–16:5

  So the churches were strengthened in the faith, and they increased in numbers daily. (Acts 16:5)

- Chapter 5: Acts 16:6–19:20

  So the word of the Lord continued to increase and prevail mightily. (Acts 19:20)

- Chapter 6: Acts 19:21–28:31

  "Therefore let it be known to you that this salvation of God has been sent to the Gentiles; they will listen." He lived [in Rome] two whole years at his own expense, and welcomed all who came to him, proclaiming the kingdom of God and teaching about the Lord Jesus Christ with all boldness and without hindrance. (Acts 28:28-31)

This is very helpful to the reader because these summary statements give us a peek into Luke's intentions and, therefore, into God's purpose for us through this God-inspired text! Luke is clearly concerned with showing the spread of the gospel and the increase and multiplication of disciples and churches. But this spread, increase and multiplication are focused in at least four ways.

First, it is focused on the spread of the gospel from Jerusalem to the ends of the earth. As the story of Acts unfolds, it is hard to miss how programmatic are the words of Jesus' commission to the disciples in Acts 1:

"But you will receive power when the Holy Spirit has

come upon you, and you will be my witnesses in Jerusalem and in all Judea and Samaria, and to the end of the earth." (Acts 1:8)

Second, Luke's history of the early church is focused on the spread of the gospel from the Jews to the Gentiles (non-Jews). As you read Acts you are going to see how difficult the transition was from being a church made up of Jews alone (Jews who believed and followed Jesus) to a church of Jews and Gentiles together. It would be difficult to overemphasize the centrality of this topic in Acts. You also see this reflected throughout the epistles.

Third, it is focused on the leaders of the Jerusalem church (primarily Peter) and on Paul. Luke shows very little interest in any of the other Apostles and their exploits.

Fourth, Luke's account is focused on how the spread of the gospel and the increase and multiplication of disciples and churches fulfills God's redemptive plan to bless the whole world through his people, a plan first revealed to Abraham and repeated throughout the entire Old Testament and the gospels:

Now the Lord said to Abram, "Go from your country and your kindred and your father's house to the land that I will show you. And I will make of you a great nation, and I will bless you and make your name great, so *that you will be a blessing.* I will bless those who bless you, and him who dishonors you I will curse, and *in you all the families of the earth shall be blessed.*" (Genesis 12:1-3; italics added)

"And all the prophets who have spoken, from Samuel and those who came after him, also proclaimed these days.

You are the sons of the prophets and of the covenant
that God made with your fathers, saying to Abraham,
'And in your offspring shall all the families of the earth be
blessed.' God, having raised up his servant, sent him to
you first, to bless you by turning every one of you from
your wickedness." (Acts 3:24-26)

God's Story, Our Story

We need this account of the spread of the gospel and the
increase of disciples and churches, starting in Jerusalem
among believing Jews and going to the ends of the earth, to
include all the nations. And by "we" I mean each one of us
individually and in community—in our church community
and in our families.

We need it because Jesus' commission to us in Acts 1:8 is
not yet complete. As we read Acts, we learn how the Holy
Spirit empowers, directs, and, you might say, drives us to
continue making disciples of all nations. You will see that the
work of the Holy Spirit is one of the most prominent themes
in this book. Thankfully, the same Holy Spirit is at work in us
and through us today. We need to know him better so we can
cooperate with his power available to us.

We need to read and understand Acts because our
understanding of the message we bear and embody is
deepened and enriched.

We need this account because, like the rest of the Bible, it
reminds us that the people and churches God uses are deeply
flawed and the road we travel as disciples is extremely
difficult, but God in his grace empowers deeply flawed
people to accomplish his purposes. We can be certain that
God will accomplish his purposes in us, through us, with us,

and in spite of us.

You and I can rejoice that we are included in the Story of God!

A Message for Those Who are Not Yet Christians

This guide assumes that the reader has made a decision to follow Christ as their forgiver and God, as Lord and Savior. It assumes you are, to use Luke's terminology, a disciple, a follower of the Way, a Christian. This assumption is especially applicable to the reflection questions starting on Week 2. So if you proceed, and I hope you do, you might want substitute the recurring reflection question from Week 1: "What stands out as being particularly helpful, insightful, or surprising in today's reading?" It is my conviction that if you pray genuinely for God to speak to you as you read through Acts, God will honor that prayer.

If you are wondering about the value of this study for your life right now, you might want to consider starting instead with my previous volume, *The Story of God: A 40-Day Guided Journey through the Bible*. It will give you a framework for the entire Bible and offer a much more comprehensive opportunity to investigate the claims of Christianity.

WEEK 1

DAY 1

🙌

Pray: Ask God to speak to you through His Word, the Bible.

You are going to read the entire book of Acts this first week. That means this week is, by far, the most challenging week for reading. But you will get so much more from the individual parts if you have the big picture in mind at the outset. Do not give up! If you struggle as a reader, you can listen to the Bible by using a Bible app on a smart phone, a tablet devise, or an online Bible site.

Today you will read "Chapter 1: Acts 1:1–6:7." Do not concern yourself with the details. This week is all about getting the overall flow of the narrative, as well as the big themes, main events, and primary players.

At the outset of Acts, Jesus is still meeting with and teaching the disciples. But after he ascends to heaven, the disciples are filled with the Holy Spirit and Peter preaches to thousands of Jews that are gathered in Jerusalem for one of the Jewish feasts (the Feast of Pentecost). Thousands respond, and the church is born.

Keep in mind that it has only been a few weeks since Jesus was crucified. The same people who crucified him are still in charge. So when the disciples continue his teaching and healing ministry, the authorities make their move and begin to persecute them. The church is mobilized to pray, God continues to work miracles through the Holy Spirit, and the church expands as more and more people become followers of Christ.

You will see how the fruit of what Jesus taught them concerning himself and their mission from the entire Scripture (our Old Testament) is bearing fruit as Peter and the disciples repeatedly refer to what has happened and what is happening as a fulfillment of Scripture. The centrality of the Bible in their ministry is obvious. Just like Jesus, they confirm the truth of their message using the Bible. The Bible is the ultimate authority. Presumably, what they imply by their use of Scripture is that if what they are doing and saying does not align with Scripture, they are not to be believed. The Bible, as the Word of God, continues to have the ultimate authority. You and I have in our possession God's revelation to us!

The "already/not yet" nature of this scene in the story of God ("Spirit") becomes evident as problems and conflicts quickly develop in the early church. [See appendix one for an overview of the 10 scenes from the Story of God.] The kingdom of God has already broken into our world through the ministry of Jesus, but it will not come in fullness until the return of Christ. Christ has won in the war against the world, the flesh, and the devil, but battles still must be fought until God's enemies are vanquished and the world is renewed in the New Creation. We (God's people) have been declared righteous, we have been sanctified (we are "saints"), and we have even been glorified in Christ (Romans 8:30), but "the flesh"—that part of us still in need of renewal and opposed to God's Spirit—is still a power to contend with. God is still working on us and he will complete his work on the day of Christ (Philippians 1:6).

Therefore God works through this flawed church and these flawed individuals found in Acts just as he does today. And the same Holy Spirit is at work today, empowering the spread of the gospel throughout the world, bringing reconciliation to people far from God, healing to the hurting, and comfort to persecuted disciples throughout the world.

Read: Acts 1:1–6:7

To get the most out of your journey, you will need to bring along a journal, a pen, and reflective posture. This week focus on jotting down impressions or verses that stand out to you as you read. Starting next week you will have questions that will help you explore the personal and corporate implications of the text.

Reflect: What stands out as being particularly helpful, insightful, or surprising in today's reading?

DAY 2

Pray: Ask God to speak to you through His Word, the Bible.

You will read two "chapters" today.
- Chapter 2: Acts 6:8–9:31
- Chapter 3: Acts 9:32–12:24

Several key turns in the story take place during these six chapters. I do not want you to miss them, so we will break up today's reading into three parts.

This first reading focuses on one of the men chosen to serve tables at the close of yesterday's reading, a man name Stephen. He becomes the first Christian martyr. The execution scene calls attention to a man name Saul who is leading a persecution against the church and who becomes the focus of much of Luke's account in Acts. Up to this point, the church's expansion has been focused on Jerusalem. But God uses the persecution to take the gospel to Judea and Samaria, as is noted at the end of this first reading.

Read Acts 6:8–8:4

Did you see the key transitions taking the gospel to Judea and Samaria? Read Acts 8:2 and 8:4 again. Jesus told them to be his witnesses, starting in Jerusalem and then going to Judea and Samaria. It is ironic that the expansion of Christ's mission beyond Jerusalem happens directly as a result of Saul's violent persecution against the spread of the gospel.

The next section describes the spread of the gospel in Samaria, to the north, and an incident where it spreads to the south of Jerusalem. But chapter 9 recounts the call of Saul the persecutor to follow Christ and serve Christ's mission, especially to the Gentile world.

Read Acts 8:5–9:31

The last reading for today (Acts 9:31–12:24) describes another dramatic turn in the narrative. God leads Peter to witness to a Gentile man named Cornelius, and the Gentile believes in Christ (together with his entire household). He is the first Gentile convert to believe and receive the Holy Spirit. God's promise to bless the nations through Abraham is finally unfolding!

Read Acts 9:31–12:24

Reflect: What stands out as being particularly helpful, insightful, or surprising in today's reading?

DAY 3

Pray: Ask God to speak to you through His Word, the Bible.

You will read two more of Luke's "chapters" today:
- Chapter 4: Acts 12:25–16:5
- Chapter 5: Acts 16:6–19:20

"Chapter 4" marks two important shifts in the narrative. The first is a shift from Jerusalem to Antioch as the center of the mission. Paul will depart from Antioch on his three missionary journeys and return there in all but the last. Most Bibles have maps that show the routes of each journey.

The second shift is from the focus on the apostles in Jerusalem (especially Peter) to Saul who is soon referred to by his Greek name, Paul, for the rest of the narrative. As the official mission to the Gentiles begins, tensions grow within the ranks of Jews who are followers of Christ. Can Gentiles become disciples of Jesus without also becoming Jews, following the Mosaic Law? The council that convenes to answer that question in Acts 15 marks a seminal moment in the mission of God.

Do not miss another dose of reality when Luke explains why Paul and Barnabas part ways at the end of chapter 15. The story has a happy ending not recorded by Luke, but the fact that this sharp disagreement is recorded offers another taste of authenticity. Because Luke is willing to record the bad and the ugly we can trust his depiction of the good!

Read: Acts 12:25–16:5

"Chapter 5" contains some of my personal favorites from Paul's journeys. He is now traveling with Silas. We see the diversity of the church in Philippi and the unusual means God uses to win over the first three sets of converts. We get a glimpse into the founding of the church in Thessalonica, Corinth, and Ephesus (all churches to whom Paul later writes multiple epistles preserved for us in the New Testament). And we see how Paul adjusts his presentation of the gospel when he preaches to the Athenians who have no knowledge of the Hebrew Scriptures. We can learn a lot from Paul's approach as we live in a world that is more and more biblically illiterate.

Read: Acts 16:6–19:20

Reflect: What stands out as being particularly helpful, insightful, or surprising in today's reading?

DAY 4

Pray: Ask God to speak to you through His Word, the Bible.

Luke's final "chapter" is long—Acts 19:21 -28:30. You will begin to read it today and wrap it up tomorrow. Paul concludes his third missionary journey in Jerusalem. He has been led there by the Holy Spirit, but it has also been prophesied that he be bound in chains, as indeed he is. The rest of the narrative recounts Paul's ministry as a prisoner of the Roman Empire as he is transferred to Rome for trial. Several of Paul's epistles were written during this period while he was in house arrest, most likely in Rome. The trip includes a shipwreck, speeches before kings and governors, and a time of extended ministry in Rome.

Read: Acts 19:22–24:27

Reflect: What stands out as being particularly helpful, insightful, or surprising in today's reading?

DAY 5

Pray: Ask God to speak to you through His Word, the Bible.

Today you conclude your first reading of Acts as you complete Luke's final "chapter." Next week we will slow down, taking the next seven weeks to explore and reflect on this amazing story of the spread of the gospel and the increase of disciples and churches, starting in Jerusalem among believing Jews and going to the ends of the earth to include all the nations.

Read: Acts 25:1–28:30

Reflect: What stands out as being particularly helpful, insightful, or

surprising in today's reading?

WEEK 2

DAY 1

Pray: Ask God to speak to you through His Word, the Bible.

Today you will read Acts 1, which begins with Luke's introduction to his second volume and a recounting of Jesus' final instructions to the disciples. As you can imagine, considering that these are final instructions, every word is packed with meaning and significance. You might want to read his final instructions more than once and reflect on the themes on which Jesus focuses. The second half of the chapter covers the disciples' first order of business: choosing a replacement for Judas.

As you read this chapter, be sure to notice key themes from the larger story of God. Unlike last week's daily readings, the majority of your time from this point onward will be spent reflecting on the story of Acts within the ongoing story of God and on your own life in light of that story. So, as you read, consider where you have seen many of the themes in Acts 1 earlier in the Story of God (e.g., God's kingdom, the nations, and the interaction between the Father, Son, and Holy Spirit).

Read: Acts 1:1-26

The disciples wonder if Jesus will now restore the kingdom to Israel:

> So when they had come together, they asked him, "Lord, will you at this time restore the kingdom to Israel?" (Acts 1:6)

They expect the new era to begin soon—the era where God rules on earth as he does in heaven. After all, Jesus asked them to pray for that day. Now he has risen from the dead. He is back, and there is so much unfinished business. Jesus, like the prophets before him in the Old Testament, spoke of a new era (a New Creation) that will be preceded by war and by God's final judgment. As the prophets gazed into the future, they could see the peaks of God's activity, but they were not able to see the valleys between those peaks.

Jesus, the Savior Messiah, will come once to suffer (peak), and then he will return to establish his kingdom rule on earth (peak). But the resurrection is not his return. His return will be from heaven. And there is a valley between the peaks. Between the Salvation scene in the story of God and the New Creation scene there is the Spirit scene. (See the Appendix.) God's kingdom has indeed broken in through Christ, but it will not come in fullness until he returns. We live in the "already/not yet" of God's kingdom rule. God's kingdom has *already* broken into the old age, but the old age is *not yet* extinct.

When the disciples ask about the kingdom, Jesus clarifies that their notion of "restoring the kingdom to Israel" is much too narrow. The end game has never been to bring glory to God by glorifying Israel. The end game is to glorify God by reaching the nations. God's plan is not simply to restore Israel, but to restore the human race and all of creation. Israel was blessed to be a blessing. Israel was given a missionary mandate. You see this in the call of Abraham and in later references to that call:

Now the Lord said to Abram, "Go from your country and your kindred and your father's house to the land that I will show you. And I will make of you a great nation, and I will bless you and make your name great, so that you will be a blessing. I will bless those who bless you, and him who dishonors you I will curse, and in you all the families of the earth shall be blessed." (Genesis 12:1-3; italics added)

"In your offspring shall all the nations of the earth be blessed, because you have obeyed my voice." (Genesis 22:18)

"Sojourn in this land, and I will be with you and will bless you, for to you and to your offspring I will give all these lands, and I will establish the oath that I swore to Abraham your father. I will multiply your offspring as the stars of heaven and will give to your offspring all these lands. And in your offspring all the nations of the earth shall be blessed." (Genesis 26:3-4; italics added)

And behold, the Lord stood above it and said, "I am the Lord, the God of Abraham your father and the God of Isaac. The land on which you lie I will give to you and to your offspring. Your offspring shall be like the dust of the earth, and you shall spread abroad to the west and to the east and to the north and to the south, and in you and your offspring shall all the families of the earth be blessed." (Genesis 28:13-14; italics added)

You even see God's larger mission reflected when God gives the law to Israel:

"See, I have taught you statutes and rules, as the Lord my God commanded me, that you should do them in the land that you are entering to take possession of it. Keep them and do them, for that will be your wisdom and your understanding *in the sight of the peoples, who, when they hear all these statutes, will say, 'Surely this great nation is a wise and understanding people.'*" (Deuteronomy 4:5-6; italics added))

The Old Testament repeatedly proclaims that the successes of Israel, including the glories of the temple, will attract people from afar to come and give glory to God. And the prophets speak often of God's mission to bless the nations.

God's mission permeates the entire Old Testament.

The opening verses of Acts 1 also feature all three members of the Trinity—it is the Father's timing; Jesus, the Son, continues to do and teach; the promised Holy Spirit will empower God's mission.

You might have remembered similar passages in the

gospels where Jesus is talking about doing the Father's will and promising his continued help and presence through the Spirit:

> "But when the Helper comes, whom I will send to you from the Father, the Spirit of truth, who proceeds from the Father, he will bear witness about me." (John 15:26)

You might also recall how all three members of the Trinity are featured at the launch of Jesus' ministry through his baptism:

> Now when all the people were baptized, and when Jesus also had been baptized and was praying, the heavens were opened, and the Holy Spirit descended on him in bodily form, like a dove; and a voice came from heaven, "You are my beloved Son; with you I am well pleased." (Luke 3:21-22)

Key themes from the story of God are featured not only here in chapter one, but also throughout the book of Acts

Reflect: Christ's mission is what you have been created, shaped, empowered, equipped, and called by God to do. The story of Acts states the mission:

> *"But you will receive power when the Holy Spirit has come upon you, and you will be my witnesses in Jerusalem and in all Judea and Samaria, and to the end of the earth." (Acts 1:8)*

It not only states the mission, it demonstrates it through this account of the early church on mission. Remember Luke's summary statements. They show Acts to be an account of the spread of the gospel and the increase of disciples and churches, starting in Jerusalem among believing Jews and going to the ends of the earth to include all the nations.

If you ask God to show you his purpose or mission for your life, do not expect him to custom-make a mission just for you. God does not custom-make a mission for your life; God custom-makes you for his mission. And he empowers you for his mission through the Spirit.

How will his mission, the Holy Spirit, and the power of the Spirit define your life?

DAY 2

Pray: Ask God to speak to you through His Word, the Bible.

Jesus tells the disciples to wait for the Spirit to come before launching the mission. About ten days after his ascension, the Holy Spirit arrives, and his arrival is unmistakable. It is a momentous event marking a new era in the story of God. It is the beginning of the Spirit scene in "Act Two" of the story of God. For those steeped in the story, what happens here is both familiar and new. It is in the familiar that what is new is magnified.

Acts 2:1-13 describes the moment the Spirit comes on the disciples of Jesus ,who are gathered and waiting on the day of Pentecost, the Jewish Festival of Weeks, that took place fifty days after Passover. As you read it, note what is familiar when compared to God's appearance to Abraham when he cut the covenant in Genesis 15:

When the sun had gone down and it was dark, behold, a

smoking fire pot and a flaming torch passed between these pieces. On that day the Lord made a covenant with Abram. (Genesis 15:17-18)

Think about the call of Moses.

And the angel of the Lord appeared to him in a flame of fire out of the midst of a bush. He looked, and behold, the bush was burning, yet it was not consumed. (Exodus 3:2)

Remember the way God showed up to the Israelites when he delivered the Ten Commandments through Moses.

And the Lord went before them by day in a pillar of cloud to lead them along the way, and by night in a pillar of fire to give them light, that they might travel by day and by night. (Exodus 13:21)

Most importantly, consider how Acts 2 recalls the day God filled the tabernacle, and the day his presence filled the temple.

Then the cloud covered the tent of meeting, and the glory of the Lord filled the tabernacle. And Moses was not able to enter the tent of meeting because the cloud settled on it, and the glory of the Lord filled the tabernacle. (Exodus 40:34-35)

As soon as Solomon finished his prayer, fire came down from heaven and consumed the burnt offering and the sacrifices, and the glory of the Lord filled the temple. And the priests could not enter the house of the Lord, because the glory of the Lord filled the Lord's house. (1

Chronicles 7:1-2)

Read Acts 2:1-13 with all this in mind and you will see how in the familiar the new is magnified.

Read: Acts 2:1-13

Reflect: What is familiar? How does that is familiar magnify what is new?

God is doing something new here. He is launching a new era. But it is a continuity of the story that has been unfolding throughout the Scriptures. God shows up in fire and smoke. His presence is manifest in wind and wonders. Unlike anything else we have seen in the story of God thus far, he is filling a group of his people with himself. The new normal will be God residing in his people. They are his tabernacle and temple. They are called to shine bright for God in a world that has rejected his rule and his love.

Reflect: You are living in the new normal where God the Holy Spirit lives in his people. His presence has filled you if you are one of his people, a follower of Christ. What difference will this make for you today as you go to work, to school, or to play among the "nations"—

among those who do not yet know God personally?

DAY 3

🖐 🖐

Pray: Ask God to speak to you through His Word, the Bible.

A crowd has gathered. Some are amazed; others are mocking. Peter addresses the crowd.

This crowd is schooled in the story of God, so Peter jumps right in, explaining how what they are witnessing is the fulfillment of something they have been waiting for as faithful Jews.

Until the day of Pentecost, the Spirit would fill certain individuals to accomplish specific missions for God. Then the Spirit would depart from that individual. But now, Peter explains, the day the Scriptures spoke of, when the Spirit would enter all of God's people and stay, had arrived. Peter quotes the prophet Joel, but Joel is not the only prophet that spoke of this.

As you read Peter's speech to the crowd, you will notice several important themes and ideas. Peter refers to this event as the beginning of the "last days." Other passages in the New Testament also refer to their day as "the last days." That means we too are living in the last days. We live in anticipation of the next big event: the return of Christ, the renewal of all things, the New Creation. This is another way of talking about the "already/not yet" nature of life between the first and second coming of Christ.

As is the nature of prophecy, one prophecy can refer to more than one future horizon or mountain peak seen in the distance. What the prophet sees as one event may actually find partial fulfillments in or near the lifetime of the prophet, in the first coming of the Christ, and in the second coming. This is the case in the Joel prophecy quoted by Peter. For all Peter knows, the events Joel prophesied but had *not yet* been fulfilled were just around the corner. But the reality is that we are still waiting even today.

Two other important themes in Peter's speech are the resurrection of Jesus and his ascension to a position of authority, honor, and power at the right hand of God.

Read: Acts 2:14-36

Reflect: It has been about fifty days since Jesus was arrested for saying things similar to what Peter is now saying. Fifty days since Peter denied Jesus three times when questioned by a servant girl. Now a large and diverse crowd of Jews from all over the Roman Empire has gathered in or near the temple courts, and Peter seizes the opportunity to speak to

them. He not only proclaims the gospel, witnessing for Jesus as instructed in Acts 1:8, but he also charges them with complicity in killing the Messiah. What has changed for Peter that he would be so bold?

If what has happened to Peter has also happened to you, what is your part now in becoming a bolder witness for Christ?

DAY 4

Pray: Ask God to speak to you through His Word, the Bible.

Peter's sermon to these devout Jews who have gathered from all over the Roman Empire contains a hard message for them to accept. Peter speaks of a crucified Messiah. No one expected that. He refers to Jesus as Lord. They would not conceive of one God in three persons. He tells them they are complicit in the killing the Messiah. No one likes to have a finger of blame pointed at them. Yet thousands are "cut to the heart" and ask Peter, "What shall we do?" How does this happen?

Read: Acts 2:37-41

Reflect: How does *this happen? How do 3000 people respond to a sermon that just days before would likely have resulted in a riot?*

The power of the Holy Spirit and the call of God on people's lives are still active today:

> "For the promise is for you and for your children and for all who are far off, everyone whom the Lord our God calls to himself." (Acts 2:39)

Every day we live, work, and play with folks whom God is calling and who may be ready to respond to the message of the gospel. We may not be called on to give a speech to thousands, but we will surely be called on to proclaim the gospel to work associates, friends, acquaintances, and family.

Reflect: How would your interactions today be different if you were aware that God might be calling the people with whom you relate to himself, and if you were confident that Holy Spirit empowers you for witness?

DAY 5

✋ ✋

Pray: Ask God to speak to you through His Word, the Bible.

We are not on our own in our witness. The Holy Spirit is with us. But so are our fellow believers. Peter is empowered by the Spirit and the other disciples flank him when he preaches at Pentecost:

> But Peter, standing with the eleven, lifted up his voice and addressed them. (Acts 2:14)

When 3000 people turn to Christ that day, the first church is founded. They form a spiritual family. Each person alone must choose Christ, but they will not follow Christ alone. Nor will they complete Christ's commission alone.

These believers gather regularly for teaching, fellowship, worship, and prayer. They not only grow deeper in their faith and in their walk with God, and stronger in their bonds to one another; they also continue together to witness and bring

more and more people into a saving knowledge of God in
Christ.

Read: Acts 2:42-47

*Reflect: As we read Acts and the epistles, it is clear that Acts 2:42 not
only describes the common life of the first church, it also summarizes
four primary practices of the church when it gathers. Why are each of
these practices essential for believers?*

Learning God's Word

Fellowship

Sharing the Lord's Supper

Prayer

Daily, as the church (God's people) live scattered in our
communities, we are called to be witnesses wherever we go.
Some Christians only think of witnessing as a solo venture.
But, as you read through Acts, you will see that the church
gathered for worship, fellowship, and service was a potent
force for witness.

Jewish historians and other writers who lived in the first
century noted that many Gentile "seekers" frequented the
synagogues throughout the Roman Empire. These "seekers"

are mentioned often in Acts and referred to as "God-fearers." We know from the epistles that "seekers" frequented church gatherings for worship. It is safe to assume that this first church in Jerusalem was effective in reaching people for Christ because they were inviting their friends and family to come, see, and experience the teaching of the Word and the life of the church gathered. Both then and now, people whom God is calling, and whose hearts are receptive to the gospel message, are intrigued by the life of a vibrant church community that is giving glory to God.

You are not alone on your mission.

WEEK 3

DAY 1

Pray: Ask God to speak to you through His Word, the Bible.

Acts 2 ends with a glowing summary of the situation: the new believers were "having favor with all the people" (Acts 2:47). Chapter 3 offers one last moment of calm before the storm of persecution from without, and then deception and dissension from within, fall on the church

Today's reading, Acts 3, recounts a healing performed by Peter through the power of Christ. Another crowd gathers in response to this miraculous event, and Peter once again seizes the opportunity to proclaim the gospel.

Read: Acts 3:1-26

Reflect: How does the content of Peter's sermon and his call to action reflect what he had learned from Jesus after the resurrection, as recorded in Luke 24?

> *Then he opened their minds to understand the Scriptures, and said to them, "Thus it is written that the Christ should suffer and on the third day rise front he dead, and that repentance and forgiveness of sins would be proclaimed in his name to all nations, beginning in Jerusalem." (Luke 24:45-47)*

Whereas Peter referred to prophecies spoken by the prophet Joel and King David in his sermon at Pentecost, here he refers to prophecies regarding a suffering Messiah and prophetic words about Jesus spoken by Moses. In addition, he reminds the crowds that all the families of the earth will be blessed through the offspring of Abraham. Again, he accuses them of complicity in killing the Messiah, but he assures them that God wants to restore them and bless them. What they need to do is repent.

Peter is drawing from the story of God as Jesus taught him and the other disciples after the resurrection. He is fulfilling the commission to preach repentance and the forgiveness of sins.

Peter also refers to the restoration of all things when Christ returns, the New Creation. God's people get a taste of what is coming now. Breaking bread together (the Lord's Supper) is a taste of the meal we will have with Jesus at the Messianic Banquet. Fellowship and worship are samples of eternity. The healings performed by Jesus and the apostles are pictures of what it will be like when all things are restored and God lives with us in the new heaven and new earth. The presence of God we experience right now, through repentance, is a foretaste of God's presence in the New Creation:

> "Repent therefore, and turn back, that your sins may be blotted out, that times of refreshing may come from the presence of the Lord." (Acts 3:19-20)

Reflect: Repentance and faith are two sides of the same coin. Repentance is turning from *sin; faith is* turning to *God. We are saved when we repent and put our faith in Christ alone. But repentance and faith are how we continue to experience the refreshment of God's presence. How is your heart straying from God lately? How will repentance and faith bring refreshment to your soul today?*

DAY 2

Pray: Ask God to speak to you through His Word, the Bible.

Now for the storm.

For three chapters the church has been experiencing good press with the outside world and unparalleled unity among themselves. All that changes beginning in chapter 4, as the church faces serious challenges from outside and inside the church. In spite of these challenges, the church continues to grow and expand. In some cases, the challenges are the primary catalyst for mission success and spiritual growth.

Peter has just healed a man who had been lame from birth and preached to a crowd that has gathered because of the miracle. But when the same religious authorities that had arrested Jesus come to investigate, they are not pleased with what Peter and John are saying.

Read: Acts 4:1-22

The resurrection is a prominent feature in Peter's sermon and in his defense. All the religious leaders would need to do to refute the resurrection is produce the body of Jesus. But they cannot. Jesus is risen.

Of course, the disciples could have hidden the body. They could be lying. However, their actions prove otherwise. They are willing to suffer and die for proclaiming the resurrection. As it has been famously stated, people may be willing to suffer and die for a lie if they are deceived by that lie, but who is willing to suffer and die and for a lie when they know it is lie?

Peter's proclamation to the religious leaders is as unpopular today as it was to these religious leaders, but for different reasons:

> "And there is salvation in no one else, for there is no other name under heaven given among men by which we must be saved." (Acts 4:12)

Jesus was God's rescue plan all along. The entire Old Testament points to him. There is no Plan B. The entire Bible proclaims what Peter says: there is no other way. But what a way it is!

God's way is the way of grace. We receive something good when we deserve something bad. Peter proclaims forgiveness is possible to the very men who arrested Jesus and handed him over to the Romans to be crucified. They did this to the Holy and Righteous One, the Author of life (Acts 3:14-15), yet these same perpetrators can be restored to him through simple repentance and faith.

God's way is available for everyone. God set out to bless all the families of the world through Abraham's offspring. God's way is not just for "good people." Salvation for good people eliminates everyone who has done something bad. And "good" is a relative term. Good compared to what or to whom? How can you ever be sure you are good enough? Besides, the Bible says God is the very definition of goodness. Only God is good, according to Jesus:

> And Jesus said to him, "Why do you call me good? No one is good except God alone." (Luke 18:19)

God's way is the relational way. We experience him and his presence by his grace. It is not about performance or perfection but by repentance and faith.

> "Repent therefore, and turn back, that your sins may be blotted out, that times of refreshing may come from the presence of the Lord." (Acts 3:19-20)

Reflect: How would you explain Peter's declaration in Acts 4:12 to a skeptic?

Read: Acts 4:23-31

Twice in this chapter, and throughout the book of Acts, the

filling of the Spirit is associated with boldness in witness:

> Then Peter, filled with the Holy Spirit, said to them, "Rulers of the people and elders." (Acts 4:8)

> They were all filled with the Holy Spirit and continued to speak the word of God with boldness. (Acts 4:31)

Reflect: How can you be bolder in sharing the gospel today?

How can you be better prepared to suffer for your faith and for sharing the gospel?

Reflecting on the believers' prayer recorded in Acts 4:24-30, how does prayer and the sovereignty of God encourage us to be bolder in our faith?

DAY 3

Pray: Ask God to speak to you through His Word, the Bible.

Read: Acts 4:32–5:11

Reflect: What do you make of the judgment on Ananias and Sapphira?

Yes, that is a hard passage to process. It is tempting to explain it away or minimize the impact. At the same time, a passage like this can be deeply misunderstood.

The nature of the misdeed is often misunderstood. Their sin is not that they kept some money to themselves from the proceeds of the land they sold. Peter makes this clear when he speaks to Ananias: "While it remained unsold, did it not remain your own? And after it was sold, was it not at your disposal?" Ananias was not compelled to contribute. Giving in the church was completely voluntary, as is seen by the commendation of Barnabas' generosity. They did not reject personal possessions or property or practice communal living. They simply considered what they had to be at the disposal of God to meet needs within the church community.

Their sin was that they lied to the Holy Spirit. They claimed to have brought all the proceeds of the land but actually kept some to themselves. Obviously God takes sin seriously. The God of the New Testament is consistent with the God of the Old Testament in both judgment and grace.

So, what do we make of this? For one thing, it is important to realize that this kind of action by God is unusual. There is nothing quite like it in the book of Acts. And while it is more frequent in the Old Testament, even there it is rare. Most misdeeds are passed over. Evil people prosper. In fact, for those who suffer under the misdeeds of powerful people, their frequent lament is with the fact that God does not bring about this kind of swift judgment more often.

It is interesting that incidents like this one happen at the outset of a movement of God. It seems God wants to make a point early on. In fact, there may be a deliberate allusion to an incident from the outset of the conquest of the land of Canaan under Joshua. The term Luke uses to describe their action—"kept back" (5:2)—is the same term used in Joshua to describe the sin of Achan (as it is translated in the Greek version of the Hebrew Bible, the version used by many in the early church). If you do not know the story, you can read about it in Joshua 7.

Could it be that God is trying to drive home a point?

The sin of Achan was repeated throughout the conquest and led to the failure of Israel to live wholeheartedly for God. What was "kept back" tempted the people to turn from God to idols for the rest of their history in the Promised Land. How much infinite pain could have been avoided if they had heeded God's bold warning, the judgment of Achan and his family?

How much damage has been done in the church, to Christians, by the posturing of God's people, pretending to be more than they are? How many people feel alone in their struggles with sin, and believe they are too defective or too unlovely to be loved by God or others, because they struggle with same sex attraction or gambling or rage or ravenous jealousy? How many Christians fail to receive the help that the body of Christ can give when we are open and vulnerable with each other about our struggles, again, because of the posturing of God's people? And how much damage has been done to the witness of the gospel in the world when Christians pretend to be better than they are?

The sin of Ananias and Sapphira is our sin. God was just in his judgment. In a very real sense it is only by God's mercy and grace that their fate is not ours. And their fate is for us a severe mercy, if we will heed its warning.

Reflect: What would it look like in the church—your church, your small groups, your Christian friendships, your family—if there was more

humility and vulnerability with one another and less posturing and pretending? What is your part in making that happen?

DAY 4

Pray: Ask God to speak to you through His Word, the Bible.

As the persecution by the authorities intensifies, the respect of the general populace deepens. God works miracles through the apostles to authenticate their message and even miraculously releases them from prison to keep the message spreading. God does not, in his sovereign wisdom and plan, spare them from being beaten, but the beating only serves to strengthen them.

Read: Acts 5:12-42

Twice now, the authorities have commanded the apostles to stop preaching. And twice Peter has declared that they must obey God rather then human beings.

The Jews and early Christians believed that the state's authority has been delegated to it by God (Romans 13:1-7). Christians are not above the laws and authorities of the land. However, when obeying the authorities would result in disobedience to God, obedience to God trumps obedience to the government or human rulers. Respect for human authorities and a willingness to disobey them when they overstep their boundaries is a theme that runs throughout the book of Acts and the rest of the New Testament.

Reflect: Why do the apostles rejoice in their suffering (Acts 5:41)?

What would need to change in your life to rejoice as they rejoiced?

DAY 5

Pray: Ask God to speak to you through His Word, the Bible.

The early church faced deception in its ranks in the incident with Ananias and Sapphira. Now it will face division in its ranks.

Read: Acts 6:1-7

Reflect: What do we learn about service in the church and priorities of ministry from this passage?

One of the seven chosen to serve tables is now the first non-apostle to face arrest and persecution.

Read: Acts 6:8-15

Reflect: Stephen was a man full of grace (Acts 6:8). How does being a person full of grace help us face injustice and persecution with peace--"his face was like the face of an angel." (Acts 6:15)?

WEEK 4

DAY 1

Pray: Ask God to speak to you through His Word, the Bible.

Stephen is the first martyr and his chief persecutor is Saul. He faces execution, reflecting the words of Jesus on the cross, and God grants him a vision of the exalted Christ before he dies.

Stephen rehearses the story of God to make a point. What seems like a recitation of facts that his hearers already know comes together to make a point at the end of his speech. It is another example of how the early Christians were now looking at the Scriptures in light of Christ.

Read: Acts 7:1–8:8

After the stoning of Stephen a great persecution breaks out

against the church in Jerusalem. The result is that they are scattered. But even more importantly, "those who were scattered went about preaching the word" (Acts 8:4). And so the gospel goes out to all Judea and Samaria:

> "But you will receive power when the Holy Spirit has come upon you, and you will be my witnesses in Jerusalem and in all Judea and Samaria." (Acts 1:8)

Reflect: Many have suggested that without the persecution that the early church in Jerusalem experienced, the believers would have stayed put in their comfort zone, Jerusalem, much longer than they should have. How is God working in your life to get you out of your comfort zone?

DAY 2

Pray: Ask God to speak to you through His Word, the Bible.

Stephen, one of the seven chosen to serve tables, has become the first Christian martyr. Philip, another one of the seven and one of the Christians scattered by the persecution, takes the gospel beyond Judea to Samaria. Then, guided by the Holy Spirit, Philip is led to a desert road south of Jerusalem to meet up with the man who would become the first non-Jewish disciple: an African man from Ethiopia.

Read: Acts 8:9-40

The region of Samaria was located in the middle of Israel, sandwiched between Judea to the south and Galilee to the north. The Samaritans were descendants of the northern tribes of Israel and had developed a form of Judaism that was considered heretical by the rest of Judaism. At one time in their history they had even built a rival temple. When the Samaritans received the gospel, it marked a new and important phase in the spread of the gospel. In a rare and unusual instance, the Spirit did not fill the new converts until apostles arrived and laid hands on them.

This served two crucial purposes. First, the Jewish believers had to accept them as brothers in Christ because of this apostolic confirmation of their faith. They were no longer seen as religious heretics or second-class Jews. Second, the Samaritans saw their link to the teaching of the apostles and to the Jewish followers of Christ in Jerusalem.

Reflect: The Ethiopian eunuch, a Gentile, just happened to be reading from Isaiah the prophet about the suffering Messiah when Philip met up with him on the road. There just happened to be a rare watering hole in this desert road out of Jerusalem when the Ethiopian man put his faith in Christ. The Holy Spirit, of course, was orchestrating this event. Philip had been summoned to a divine appointment. Do you believe the Spirit is creating divine appointments in your life with people who are far from God? Why or why not? If so, what do you need to do today to be more aware of a divine appointment?

DAY 3

☙ ☙

Pray: Ask God to speak to you through His Word, the Bible.

The gospel had spread from Jerusalem to Judea and Samaria and even south, we can presume, through the witness of the Ethiopian eunuch. The events of chapters 9–12 prepare the church for the next expansion leading to Rome and beyond. The first order of business is a radical change for the man who is leading the persecution of believers, the man who would become known as the "apostle to the Gentiles."

> But the Lord said to [Ananias], "Go, for [Saul] is a chosen instrument of mine to carry my name before the Gentiles and kings and the children of Israel. For I will show him how much he must suffer for the sake of my name." (Acts 9:15-16)

After Paul's call, Luke records a remarkable event in the life of Peter that would prove crucial in defining the nature of the mission to the Gentiles.

The call of the persecutor Saul to follow Christ is recounted in today's reading. It is so important, and such a watershed moment in the Christian mission, that his calling is told three times in Acts. Saul (also known as Paul) is the main figure from chapter 13 onward in Acts.

Read: Acts 9:1-31

When the risen Christ confronted Saul on the road to Damascus, he made the point twice that Saul was persecuting *him*:

> "Saul, Saul, why are you persecuting me?" And he said, "Who are you, Lord?" And he said, "I am Jesus, whom you are persecuting. (Acts 9:4-5)

Jesus so identifies with his church that to persecute the church is to persecute him. This lesson was not lost on Paul. Later in his ministry, writing to the church in Corinth, he declared to them, "Now you are the body of Christ and individually members of it" (1 Corinthians 12:27).

While Saul's call to follow Christ is quite unique, there are elements in common with most conversions in the Bible. Most importantly, there is God's initiative and the role of other believers. Saul heard the gospel directly from Jesus, but Ananias and Barnabas soon played an important role in his first steps as a follower of Christ. And, like Saul, all who respond to God's call are called to mission. We may not be called to preach to kings, but we are called to be witnesses for Christ.

Reflect: Write a prayer for someone you know and whom you consider to be one of the most unlikely candidates to turn to Christ and become an effective leader in the church.

DAY 4

Pray: Ask God to speak to you through His Word, the Bible.

Now Luke turns to Peter's ministry beyond Jerusalem.

Read: Acts 9:32-43

The way Luke tells the story of Acts reminds us from time to time that not every disciple of Jesus is called to travel the globe, preaching to kings and healing the sick. Nevertheless, he also highlights how every disciple's life and ministry counts before God. One of those disciples who counted before God was Tabitha:

> Now there was in Joppa a disciple named Tabitha, which, translated, means Dorcas. She was full of good works and

acts of charity. (Acts 9:36)

Paul was an adventurer, but he did not expect everyone to express their faith as he did, with a sort of wild abandon, walking directly into situations that he knew would result in beatings and imprisonment, if not death. His counsel for the believers in the city of Thessalonica seems tame, but it reminds us of Luke's description above of Tabitha's life and ministry:

> Now concerning brotherly love you have no need for anyone to write to you, for you yourselves have been taught by God to love one another, for that indeed is what you are doing to all the brothers throughout Macedonia. But we urge you, brothers, to do this more and more, and to aspire to live quietly, and to mind your own affairs, and to work with your hands, as we instructed you, so that you may walk properly before outsiders and be dependent on no one. (1 Thessalonians 4:9-12)

Reflect: Your example alone will not serve as a witness for Christ. To witness to something requires words. Witnessing for Christ requires words. But your example and conduct—the love you express to others— will enhance your words of witness. How can you live a life today full of good works, acts of charity, and walking properly before outsiders? What will that look like in your daily life?

DAY 5

Pray: Ask God to speak to you through His Word, the Bible.

Now comes the event that will pave the way for Paul's ministry to the Gentiles. Interestingly, the event features Peter.

Read: Acts 10:1–11:18

Luke devotes more words to this event than any other single event in Acts. God is unveiling one of the most revolutionary implications of the gospel: Gentiles will be admitted into the kingdom based on faith in Christ alone, plus nothing else. They receive the Spirit without first becoming Jews through circumcision:

While Peter was still saying these things, the Holy Spirit

fell on all who heard the word. And the believers from among the circumcised who had come with Peter were amazed, because the gift of the Holy Spirit was poured out even on the Gentiles. For they were hearing them speaking in tongues and extolling God. Then Peter declared, "Can anyone withhold water for baptizing these people, who have received the Holy Spirit just as we have?" (Acts 10:44-47)

Reflect: It is difficult to see our own biases and prejudices. We find ways to rationalize and justify them. The Jews were given laws that made them live distinctive lives. They were called to be holy in an unholy world. But they were also called to bless the world and reach it for God. However, many used the law to justify prejudices and biases against those who were part of their mission to reach for God.

Christians are prone to do the same thing. Even though it is hard to see this in ourselves, are there people whom you hesitate to love and whom you avoid and dislike because of their lifestyle, nationality, religion, race, or any other factor? Ask God to reveal what is in your heart and then confess it to God, asking him to give you a vision of his love and his desire to spread salvation to everyone.

WEEK 5

DAY 1

Pray: Ask God to speak to you through His Word, the Bible.

Luke once again notes the missional consequences of the scattering that happened as a result of the persecution in Jerusalem. Most who scattered preached solely to Jews, but a smaller group began to proclaim the gospel to non-Jews in Antioch and received a great response. The Jerusalem leaders dispatch Barnabas to check things out and Barnabas, the son of encouragement, seeks out Saul, bringing him to Antioch and ministering with him side-by-side.

Read: Acts 11:19-30

Reflect: Many who spread the gospel in Acts are anonymous:

> *Men of Cyprus and Cyrene, who on coming to Antioch spoke to the Hellenists also, preaching the Lord Jesus. And the hand of the Lord was with them, and a great number who believed turned to the Lord. (Acts 11:20-21)*

> *We know of Phillip's outreach to the Ethiopian eunuch. Peter's encounter with Cornelius is well documented. But we know next to nothing about these men from Cyprus and Cyrene who were early pioneers, forging new roads for the gospel among the Gentiles. God is well aware of who they were. How do you feel when no one but God seems to remember your ministry efforts?*

DAY 2

Pray: Ask God to speak to you through His Word, the Bible.

There is more than one Herod in the New Testament. Acts 12 recounts the exploits of Herod Agrippa I, the grandson of Herod the Great (the Herod from the Christmas story). Herod Agrippa I is a nephew of Herod Antipas, the Herod who beheaded John the Baptist and who questioned Jesus after his arrest.

There are two James' of note in the New Testament. One is the disciple of Jesus, the brother of John the disciple. He was part of Jesus' inner circle of disciples, which also included Peter and John. The other James is the brother of Jesus who assumed the key leadership role over the church in Jerusalem. The first James, the disciple of Jesus, is the James of Acts 12.

As you read the account of Peter's miraculous escape from prison, note the extra amount of detail and humor in the narrative.

Read: Acts 12:1-24

Reflect: What do you think of the fact that God rescues Peter but he does not rescue James?

DAY 3

Pray: Ask God to speak to you through His Word, the Bible.

The opening verses of Acts 13 mark an important point in church history—the first instance of a church sending out missionaries. Chapters 13–14 record this first missionary journey.

This first missionary movement is birthed in worship and fasting and led by the Holy Spirit. In fact, the initiative of the Holy Spirit is repeated for emphasis. World missions is God's idea:

> While they were worshiping the Lord and fasting, the Holy Spirit said, "Set apart for me Barnabas and Saul for the work to which I have called them." (Acts 13:2)

> Then after fasting and praying they laid their hands on them and sent them off. (Acts 13:4)

From this point on, Saul (now going by his Roman name, Paul) will be the primary figure in Acts.

Read: Acts 12:25–13:52

Paul's sermon once again recounts the story of God. This theme, that the whole Bible pointed to Christ *and* to the mission of God to redeem the whole world, is central to Acts. Paul's quotation of Isaiah is just one more way of making the point that the mission of God was always about reaching the nations:

> "I have made you a light for the Gentiles, that you may bring salvation to the ends of the earth."(Acts 13:47)

Reflect: Luke's gospel has a special emphasis on prayer, including several stories, teachings, and references to prayer not found in the other gospels. That emphasis continues in his account of the early church:

> *All these with one accord were devoting themselves to prayer, together with the women and Mary the mother of Jesus, and his brothers. (Acts 1:14)*

> *And they devoted themselves to the apostles' teaching and the fellowship, to the breaking of bread and the prayers. (Acts 2:42)*

> *And when they had prayed, the place in which they were gathered*

together was shaken, and they were all filled with the Holy Spirit and continued to speak the word of God with boldness. (Acts 4:31)

At Caesarea there was a man named Cornelius, a centurion of what was known as the Italian Cohort, a devout man who feared God with all his household, gave alms generously to the people, and prayed continually to God. (Acts 10:1-2)

The next day, as they were on their journey and approaching the city, Peter went up on the housetop about the sixth hour to pray. (Acts 10:9)

So Peter was kept in prison, but earnest prayer for him was made to God by the church. (Acts 12:5)

Why does corporate prayer play an important role in the life of believer and the church?

Why does corporate prayer play an important role in the life of every believer and every church?

DAY 4

Pray: Ask God to speak to you through His Word, the Bible.

Chapter 14 recounts the rest of first missionary journey. You will notice how Paul adjusts his message when he speaks to Gentiles who are not already God-fearers and, thus, already familiar with the story of God.

Read: Acts 14

God has a plan to redeem the world, both Jews and Gentiles. God is also at work to bring the world to himself:

> And when the Gentiles heard this, they began rejoicing and glorifying the word of the Lord, and as many as were appointed to eternal life believed. (Acts 13:48)

And when they arrived and gathered the church together, they declared all that God had done with them, and *how he had opened a door of faith* to the Gentiles. (Acts 14:27; italics added)

The fact that God has a plan and God is at work could be reason to avoid risk. After all, God will accomplish his plan with or without you or me. Right? Not so for Paul and Barnabas. They repeatedly walk into danger in order to live out God's plan and do God's work. After being stoned and left for dead, Paul gets up and travels over sixty miles to Derbe to preach some more.

Reflect: There are risks involved with sharing our faith with friends, co-workers and family. How does Paul's example encourage you to be bolder in sharing your faith?

DAY 5

Pray: Ask God to speak to you through His Word, the Bible.

The Gentiles are responding to the gospel in growing numbers. In spite of Peter's experience with Cornelius, there is a faction that is teaching the necessity of circumcision for salvation. They come to Antioch where Paul and Barnabas engage them in vigorous debate. It becomes evident that circumcision is only the beginning for this faction. The goal is have all Christians also live under the Law of Moses. So Paul, Barnabas and a delegation from Antioch (the center of the Christian mission) go down to Jerusalem to consult with the apostles and elders regarding this situation.

Read: Acts 15

It is interesting that right after this show of unity, recorded in Acts 15:1-35, Paul and Barnabas have a sharp disagreement and decide to part ways because they can not agree on whether John Mark should accompany them on the next missionary journey. It is a reminder that God uses broken vessels to carry his message. Luke, once again, does not shrink back from sharing the good, the bad and the ugly. Fortunately, Paul's epistles suggest that Paul, Barnabas and John Mark eventually reconciled (1 Corinthians 9:6; Colossians 4:10; 2 Timothy 4:11).

God himself gave the law, but its purpose of providing special rules for living had come to an end. It still reveals God's character and his goodness. In matters of ethics, it still reveals what is right and wrong. But in Christ we are now saved by and live in God's grace revealed in Christ.

Paul's epistles, especially Galatians, are proof that this council in Jerusalem did not settle the issue. Many continued to insist that Gentiles must live under the law. But Peter is insistent that salvation is by grace alone:

> "But we believe that we will be saved through the grace of the Lord Jesus, just as they will." (Acts 15:11)

Reflect: Many Christians today continue to place burdens on other Christians that find their origin in the law or church traditions. It is natural for churches, families, and Christian organizations to have "house rules," but these should not be associated with salvation, growing in holiness, or Christian identity. It is tempting to take our "house

rules" too far. If you think about it, it is easier to point to rules than to point to the necessities of love, the guidance of the Holy Spirit, and the transforming power of the Spirit to overcome sin in our lives. What "house rules" do you tend to associate with salvation?

How are you depending on these biblical dynamics of gospel for your growth as a follower of Christ?

WEEK 6

DAY 1

Pray: Ask God to speak to you through His Word, the Bible.

Paul has set out on his second missionary journey. Acts 16 chronicles the founding of a church that would have a long and intimate relationship with Paul for the rest of his ministry, the church in Philippi. This chapter also details the growing diversity of the church as it spread throughout the Roman world.

Read: Acts 16

Picture it: Paul persuading a group of women on the banks of a river. Imagine the moment Paul turns and in his frustration casts a demon out of a slave girl. See Paul and Silas bloodied and in stocks in a dingy prison, singing songs of praise at the top of their lungs. Now think about Paul and Silas, recently released from prison, worshipping at the home of a wealthy, world-traveling businesswoman, surrounded by Lydia's friends, her household, a former slave girl, and a Roman jailer.

About seven years have elapsed the next time this church is specifically mentioned in the story of God. Paul writes a letter thanking the church at Philippi for a financial gift they sent while he was under house arrest, also mentioning their financial partnership throughout his ministry:

> And you Philippians yourselves know that in the beginning of the gospel, when I left Macedonia, no church entered into partnership with me in giving and receiving, except you only. Even in Thessalonica you sent me help for my needs once and again. Not that I seek the gift, but I seek the fruit that increases to your credit. I have received full payment, and more. I am well supplied, having received from Epaphroditus the gifts you sent, a fragrant offering, a sacrifice acceptable and pleasing to God. And my God will supply every need of yours according to his riches in glory in Christ Jesus. To our God and Father be glory forever and ever. Amen. (Philippians 4:15-20)

Most of the members in this church never traveled the world. Day in and day out, they simply went to work and did it all for God's glory. They fellowshipped, served, and shared their faith with their family and neighbors. Most of these folks with whom they shared their faith rejected them. But they were committed to God, to each other, and to the gospel. Lydia, the slave girl, the jailor, and the undoubtedly ragtag group that formed around them changed the course of human history by partnering with Paul in his mission. Even you and I owe part of our spiritual legacy to them because of their support of Paul's ministry.

Reflect: How are you partnering with others to impact the world for Christ?

DAY 2

Pray: Ask God to speak to you through His Word, the Bible.

When Paul and his missionary companions arrive at Thessalonica, they continue their practice of going to the synagogue and sharing the gospel:

> He reasoned with them from the Scriptures, explaining and proving that it was necessary for the Christ to suffer and to rise from the dead, and saying, "This Jesus, whom I proclaim to you, is the Christ." (Acts 17:2-3)

As usual, for the most part, the God-fearers who attend the synagogue respond well, and most of the Jews do not.

Paul's two epistles to the Thessalonians, preserved in the New Testament, witness to the strength of the church Paul founded in that city. Yet Paul's stay is short ("three Sabbaths") because his opponents drive him out of the city. The stay in Philippi seemed to be even shorter.

How did these churches and new believers in Macedonia continue to thrive? We know, of course, that Paul corresponded with these churches, and they would at times send emissaries to Paul (e.g., the Philippians sent Epaphroditus to Paul in prison as he notes in Philippians 4:18). Some Macedonians even traveled with Paul in his later travels (Acts 19:29; 20:4). Paul also returned to these churches on future journeys (Acts 20:1-2). But most importantly, Paul would send his missionary companions (Silas, Timothy, and others) to continue training and ministering to these young disciples (Acts 18:5; 19:22).

Read: Acts 17:1-15

Reflect: The Berean Jews

> *were more noble than those in Thessalonica; they received the word with all eagerness, examining the Scriptures daily to see if these things were so. (Acts 17:11)*

How can you demonstrate the qualities leading to this kind of nobility?

What have been some of the primary means God has used to train you in discipleship?

DAY 3

Pray: Ask God to speak to you through His Word, the Bible.

Athens had lost much of its ancient splendor by the time Paul arrived. But it was still a hotbed of philosophical interest, as noted by Luke: "Now all the Athenians and the foreigners who lived there would spend their time in nothing except telling or hearing something new" (Acts 17:21). In Lystra (Acts 14:15-17), Paul adapted his proclamation of the gospel to the audience who does not know anything about the God of the Bible:

> "Men, why are you doing these things? We also are men, of like nature with you, and we bring you good news, that you should turn from these vain things to a living God, who made the heaven and the earth and the sea and all that is in them. In past generations he allowed all the nations to walk in their own ways. Yet he did not leave

himself without witness, for he did good by giving you rains from heaven and fruitful seasons, satisfying your hearts with food and gladness." (Acts 14:15-16)

He does not quote the Bible, nor does he assume knowledge of the story of God in the Bible.

Note the similarities between this address and the one in Athens as you read Luke's account of Paul preaching to Gentiles in Athens.

Read: Acts 17:16-34

Reflect: List the cultural references Paul used and the big ideas he communicated to the Athenians. How might you communicate Christ and his resurrection to someone who is biblically illiterate?

DAY 4

Pray: Ask God to speak to you through His Word, the Bible.

In this chapter we read about the founding of one of the most notorious churches in the New Testament as evidenced by Paul's correspondence preserved in the New Testament—the first and second epistles to the Corinthians.

Corinth is Paul's last major stop on his second missionary journey. For a year and a half he resides there, teaching the Word to those who are receptive.

We are also introduced to a married couple that became important partners with Paul in ministry, Aquila and Priscilla (Romans 16:3; 1 Corinthians 16:19; 2 Timothy 4:19).

Read: Acts 18:1-22

Acts 18:3 is the only reference to Paul's trade. It is his primary way of earning a living during his travels, aside from occasional donations from some of the churches he founded. While Paul's trade is not mentioned elsewhere, he does refer to working outside of vocational ministry to earn his living in two of his epistles:

> For you remember, brothers, our labor and toil: we worked night and day, that we might not be a burden to any of you, while we proclaimed to you the gospel of God. (1 Thessalonians 2:9)

> Or is it only Barnabas and I who have no right to refrain from working for a living? (1 Corinthians 9:6)

Reflect: "Tentmaking" is a term used today to describe missionaries who earn a living outside of vocational ministry while on the mission field rather than receiving a salary from individual donors, a church, or a Christian organization. In a very real sense, we are all "tentmakers," being on mission where we live and work. What would change in your life if you saw yourself as a self-supporting missionary sent by God to your workplace, neighborhood, or school?

DAY 5

❦ ❦

Pray: Ask God to speak to you through His Word, the Bible.

Paul departs on his third journey starting in Acts 18:23, a journey that will take him to Jerusalem where he will be arrested and eventually transferred to Rome for trial. Acts 19 covers his ministry in Ephesus, which had a far-reaching impact in that region:

> But when some became stubborn and continued in unbelief, speaking evil of the Way before the congregation, he withdrew from them and took the disciples with him, reasoning daily in the hall of Tyrannus. This continued for two years, so that all the residents of Asia heard the word of the Lord, both Jews and Greeks. (Acts 19:9-10)

All told, his ministry in Ephesus totaled nearly three years!

Acts 19:21 outlines what is essentially the rest of Paul's

ministry leading to his imprisonment:

> Now after these events Paul resolved in the Spirit to pass
> through Macedonia and Achaia and go to Jerusalem,
> saying, "After I have been there, I must also see
> Rome." (Acts 19:21)

Read: Acts 18:23–19:41

The disciples carry on Jesus' frontal attack on Satan and his
kingdom through exorcism. Aside from this display of
demonic power here in chapter 19 and in chapter 16
(regarding the slave girl in Philippi), there are at least two
other references to exorcisms in Acts:

> The people also gathered from the towns around
> Jerusalem, bringing the sick and those afflicted with
> unclean spirits, and they were all healed. (Acts 5:16)

> For unclean spirits, crying out with a loud voice, came out
> of many who had them, and many who were paralyzed or
> lame were healed. (Acts 8:7)

The apostles and Jesus could have spent all their time
healing the sick and casting out demons, but they did not.
Proclaiming the gospel of the kingdom took precedence over
demonstrating it through signs and wonders if we are to
judge by the ratio of preaching to healing. In fact, instances
of miraculous healing and exorcism are few and far between
in light of what could have been. Here, in Ephesus, a center
of ancient magical practices, exorcisms and displays of

demonic power play a strategic role in the spread of the gospel in that region. Apparently Jesus and the apostles healed the sick and exorcised demons only when led to do so by the Holy Spirit.

Reflect: We are called to both proclaim the gospel of the kingdom and demonstrate it through acts of mercy and kindness. How are these two ministries evident in your own life?

WEEK 7

DAY 1

Pray: Ask God to speak to you through His Word, the Bible.

For all the historical details contained in Acts, most of what happened in the early days of the church went unchronicled. Take, for instance, the opening verses of Acts 20:

> After the uproar ceased, Paul sent for the disciples, and after encouraging them, he said farewell and departed for Macedonia. When he had gone through those regions and had given them much encouragement, he came to Greece. There he spent three months, and when a plot was made against him by the Jews as he was about to set sail for Syria, he decided to return through Macedonia. (Acts 20:1-3)

Those three short verses cover months of ministry. During that time, Paul writes two of his longest epistles. 2 Corinthians was likely written while he ministered on his way to Greece. Then, arriving in Greece (most likely in Corinth), he remains there three months and writes his masterpiece, the epistle to the Romans. Reading 2 Corinthians and Romans offers many important details about Paul's ministry and his plans as he traveled to Rome, most of which goes unreported by Luke.

Instead, Luke focuses on Paul's traveling companions, which include many members from the churches he planted in that region. In addition, Luke recounts a fascinating incident when a young man named Eutychus falls asleep while Paul is preaching. Then, in one of the most emotionally charged passages in Acts, Luke conveys Paul's final words to the Ephesian elders.

Read: Acts 20

Reflect: Take the time necessary to detail Paul's understanding of what is involved in church leadership, drawing from his words to the Ephesian elders.

How does this inform your understanding of leadership and influence in all arenas of life?

DAY 2

Pray: Ask God to speak to you through His Word, the Bible.

Paul finally arrives in Jerusalem in Acts 21. Within a week of arriving, on one of his visits to the temple, Paul is spotted by a group of Jews from Asia who stir up the crowd against Paul. They seize him and begin to beat him, but he escapes death when a Roman contingent of soldiers quickly move in to break up the mob. This is what Paul expected, as he told the Ephesian elders in chapter 20:

> "And now, behold, I am going to Jerusalem, constrained by the Spirit, not knowing what will happen to me there, except that the Holy Spirit testifies to me in every city that imprisonment and afflictions await me. But I do not account my life of any value nor as precious to myself, if only I may finish my course and the ministry that I received from the Lord Jesus, to testify to the gospel of

the grace of God." (Acts 20:22-24)

Read: Acts 21:1-36

Luke often records, without comment, events that are perplexing to us. Two such events occur in these verses.

In verse 4, Luke informs us that the disciples in Tyre were telling Paul, "through the Spirit" (no less), not to go to Jerusalem. Yet Paul testified to the Ephesian elders that he was "constrained by the Spirit" to go to Jerusalem. Apparently, Paul did not believe the Spirit was had changed his mind. Either Paul was convinced that these disciples were incorrectly labeling their personal misgivings as being from the Spirit, or they are misinterpreting what the Spirit was actually saying. Perhaps the Spirit was saying that Paul would face imprisonment or persecution (as Agabus prophecies in verse 10), and they misinterpreted it as a sign not to go. Whatever the case, we do not know the answer.

We do know that Paul cautions the believers in Thessalonica to respect, but to test, such proclamations of God's will by fellow believers (1 Thessalonians 5:19-20). Maybe they have indeed received a prompting or leading from the Holy Spirit. In such cases, we have no better test than to hold these promptings up to the truth found in Scripture. Beyond that, we can ask other believers for their advice and their prayers. Ultimately, when the Scripture does not offer clear direction, each person must discern for themselves what they will do, just as Paul did.

The other perplexing event that is recorded without comment occurs on Paul's arrival to Jerusalem. The leaders explain that Paul can win points with Jewish Christians in Jerusalem, who are zealous for the law and are upset that Paul does not require Gentiles to be circumcised or live by the law. Just how far Paul went with this is illustrated in Galatians, writing to Gentile Christians who are considering circumcision and law-keeping:

> For freedom Christ has set us free; stand firm therefore, and do not submit again to a yoke of slavery. Look: I, Paul, say to you that if you accept circumcision, Christ will be of no advantage to you. I testify again to every man who accepts circumcision that he is obligated to keep the whole law. You are severed from Christ, you who would be justified by the law; you have fallen away from grace. For through the Spirit, by faith, we ourselves eagerly wait for the hope of righteousness. For in Christ Jesus neither circumcision nor uncircumcision counts for anything, but only faith working through love. (Galatians 5:1-6)

In spite of this conviction, Paul has Timothy, whose mother was Jewish, circumcised in Acts 16:3, and, here in Acts 21, he takes what seems to be a Nazarite vow (see Numbers 6:1-21). Luke makes no comment on these apparent inconsistencies, but we get some insight directly from Paul in 1 Corinthians:

> For though I am free from all, I have made myself a servant to all, that I might win more of them. To the Jews I became as a Jew, in order to win Jews. To those under the law I became as one under the law (though not being myself under the law) that I might win those under the

law. To those outside the law I became as one outside the law (not being outside the law of God but under the law of Christ) that I might win those outside the law. To the weak I became weak, that I might win the weak. I have become all things to all people, that by all means I might save some. I do it all for the sake of the gospel, that I may share with them in its blessings. (1 Corinthians 9:19-23)

Reflect: Paul is willing to follow the Spirit into dangerous situations and to set aside his own rights for the sake of winning others to Christ. If God's mission is your primary agenda for today, how will your interactions with others, the way you do your work, your prayer life, and all other aspects of this day reflect this primary concern?

DAY 3

Pray: Ask God to speak to you through His Word, the Bible.

Paul addresses the crowd in the temple. First, he establishes his credentials and, in so doing, identifies with the concerns of his hearers. Then he shares his own testimony regarding what happened on the road to Damascus.

Read: Acts 21:37–22:29

The crowd erupts again at the mention of his mission to the Gentiles. Luke indicates this is the breaking point in verse 22:

> "And [Jesus] said to me [i.e., Paul], 'Go, for I will send you far away to the Gentiles.'" Up to this word they listened to him. Then they raised their voices and said, "Away with such a fellow from the earth! For he should not be

allowed to live." (Acts 22:21-22).

The tragedy is that the people of Israel were called for this very task--to bless the nations.

Reflect: Sadly, many Christians today forget their mission to be Christ's witnesses, locally and globally. Some are prone to criticize and attack churches and individuals who prioritize gospel proclamation. Why do so many believers do this, and what do you think they have in common with those who attacked Paul that day?

How can you keep from forgeting your mission to reach others for Christ?

DAY 4

Pray: Ask God to speak to you through His Word, the Bible.

The Roman tribune presents Paul to the Jewish leadership in Jerusalem in order to discover what has riled the Jews in the temple. Paul presents his defense.

Read: Acts 22:30–23:11

Luke emphasizes Paul's shrewdness before the tribune in chapter 21, and then, again, when he appears before the council. The scene recalls Jesus' words in Matthew:

> "Behold, I am sending you out as sheep in the midst of wolves, so be wise as serpents and innocent as doves." (Matthew 10:16)

Then Jesus goes on to offer instruction for situations identical to Paul's in Acts 23:

"Beware of men, for they will deliver you over to courts and flog you in their synagogues, and you will be dragged before governors and kings for my sake, to bear witness before them and the Gentiles. When they deliver you over, do not be anxious how you are to speak or what you are to say, for what you are to say will be given to you in that hour. For it is not you who speak, but the Spirit of your Father speaking through you. Brother will deliver brother over to death, and the father his child, and children will rise against parents and have them put to death, and you will be hated by all for my name's sake. But the one who endures to the end will be saved." (Matthew 10:17-22)

Reflect: Where in your life right now are you needing to be as wise as a serpent and innocent as a dove? How can you grow in these characteristics?

DAY 5

Pray: Ask God to speak to you through His Word, the Bible.

After Jesus calls Paul on the road to Damascus, he tells Ananias that Paul will testify before kings:

> But the Lord said to him, "Go, for he is a chosen instrument of mine to carry my name before the Gentiles and kings and the children of Israel." (Acts 9:15)

The night Paul is taken back to the barracks after appearing before the Jewish council, Jesus appears to him in a vision and assures Paul that he will make it to Rome:

> The following night the Lord stood by him and said, "Take courage, for as you have testified to the facts about me in Jerusalem, so you must testify also in Rome." (Acts 23:11)

The following events recounted in Acts 23:12-35 propel those two promises forward.

Realistically, speaking before kings and traveling to Rome as a prisoner would not be Paul's preferred means of achieving God's goal, but it was the means God had chosen.

We can see the Lord sovereignly working out his plan throughout the rest of this chapter, even though he is not mentioned again after verse 11, where he assures Paul that he will testify in Rome. But the Lord's assurance makes clear that nothing is happening that catches him by surprise, and he will work out the details of every step of his redemptive plan in spite of human sin and willfulness.

Read: Acts 23:12-35.

Reflect: How might you become more aware of God's sovereign plan working out in your life even when circumstances are difficult and you cannot sense God's presence?

How can you grow in accepting God's means for accomplishing his mission through you when his means are difficult or uncomfortable?

WEEK 8

DAY 1

Pray: Ask God to speak to you through His Word, the Bible.

Paul arrives in Caesarea during the night, and later appears before the governor, Felix, and his accusers, Jewish leaders who traveled there from Jerusalem.

After hearing both sides, Felix puts off judgment but summons Paul so, together with his Jewish wife, he can speak privately with Paul. Luke describes Felix's response:

> And as [Paul] reasoned about righteousness and self-control and the coming judgment, Felix was alarmed and said, "Go away for the present. When I get an opportunity I will summon you." (Acts 24:25)

Two years of house arrest ensue, although Paul is allowed visitors to take care of his needs.

Read: Acts 24

In his defense before Felix and his accusers, Paul claimed that he was a true Jew, holding to everything laid down in Scripture. In a very real sense, Paul never "converted" to Christianity but was "called" to follow Christ by the same God in whom he had always believed and whom he had always followed. Accordingly, Paul urged his fellow Jews to accept Jesus as the promised Messiah:

> "But this I confess to you, that according to the Way, which they call a sect, I worship the God of our fathers, believing everything laid down by the Law and written in the Prophets, having a hope in God, which these men themselves accept, that there will be a resurrection of both the just and the unjust." (Acts 24:14-15)

Reflect: Paul "reasoned about righteousness and self-control and the coming judgment" with Felix (Acts 24:25). Why do you think this alarmed Felix? Why would these subjects alarm many people today?

Reflect on your willingness or struggle to speak about biblical truths that might be alarming to people who are far from God.

DAY 2

Pray: Ask God to speak to you through His Word, the Bible.

Paul continues to be as wise as a serpent and innocent as a dove. Jesus has told him in a vision that he will make it to Rome. Yet Paul is not passive before his accusers. Nor does he simply let go and let God make all the arrangements for his journey.

Read: Acts 25

Reflect: When we are to "let go and let God" or to take action is not spelled out in this passage. In fact, it is not spelled out in any passage as

a once for all rule or procedure. What the Bible teaches us is that we must discern, on a case-by-case basis, whether we are to let events simply unfold without taking action or attempt to shape events. And we know that both courses are possible and both can be honoring to God. How can you ensure that you are spiritually discerning which course to take at critical junctures in your life and not simply following your natural inclinations?

> *And it is my prayer that your love may abound more and more, with knowledge and all discernment, so that you may approve what is excellent, and so be pure and blameless for the day of Christ, filled with the fruit of righteousness that comes through Jesus Christ, to the glory and praise of God. (Philippians 1:9-11)*

> *I appeal to you therefore, brothers, by the mercies of God, to present your bodies as a living sacrifice, holy and acceptable to God, which is your spiritual worship. Do not be conformed to this world, but be transformed by the renewal of your mind, that by testing you may discern what is the will of God, what is good and acceptable and perfect. (Romans 12:1-2)*

DAY 3

Paul makes his defense before King Agrippa and Festus. In so doing, Paul's faith story is recounted for the third time in Acts. The fact that Luke does not merely summarize it, but rather includes it three times, points to its vital importance.

Paul's faith story has three parts and two essential elements that can be clearly discerned.

Part 1: Paul tells the story of this life before Christ:

"I myself was convinced that I ought to do many things in opposing the name of Jesus of Nazareth. And I did so in Jerusalem." (Acts 26:9-10)

Part 2: Paul describes the moment his eyes are opened and he comes to faith in Christ. Paul's case is quite dramatic, but every time someone receives Christ it is a miraculous event. No one's story is truly undramatic, even if they received Christ as a child in a Sunday school class or during bedtime prayers with their parents:

"At midday, O king, I saw on the way a light from heaven, brighter than the sun, that shone around me and those who journeyed with me. And when we had all fallen to the ground, I heard a voice saying to me in the Hebrew language, 'Saul, Saul, why are you persecuting me? It is hard for you to kick against the goads.' And I said, 'Who are you, Lord?' And the Lord said, 'I am Jesus whom you are persecuting.'" (Acts 26:13-15)

Part 3: Paul tells of his life since receiving Christ. He has gone from persecutor of Christians to preacher of the gospel.

The two essential elements in a faith story are a presentation of the gospel and an explanation of how to receive what God has done for us in Christ (i.e., by repenting and believing in Christ):

"So I stand here testifying both to small and great, saying nothing but what the prophets and Moses said would come to pass: that the Christ must suffer and that, by being the first to rise from the dead, he would proclaim light both to our people and to the Gentiles." (Acts 26:22-23)

"That they should repent and turn to God, performing deeds in keeping with their repentance." (Acts 26:20)

Read: Acts 26

For Paul, salvation is about grace and God's work of forgiveness from first to last. We are not only forgiven and made right by God's grace through faith; we are also made holy (i.e., sanctified) by grace through faith. He clearly explains that those who receive Christ repent of their former lives and evidence a changed life:

> "That they should repent and turn to God, performing deeds in keeping with their repentance." (Acts 26:20)

> "To open their eyes, so that they may turn from darkness to light and from the power of Satan to God, that they may receive forgiveness of sins and a place among those who are sanctified by faith in me." (Acts 26:18)

Reflect: Take the time necessary to write out your own faith story including all three parts and both essential elements.

DAY 4

Pray: Ask God to speak to you through His Word, the Bible.

If you suffering from seasickness you may want to skip this chapter! Luke goes into great detail describing a sea voyage and a harrowing storm at sea, apparently having experienced it with Paul, as indicated by his first person plural account.

Read: Acts 27

Reflect: Once again, even though Paul has been assured in a vision that everything will work out, he takes action in line with God's plan. In doing so, Paul takes a leadership role in this crisis at sea. How can you

be ready to bring spiritual leadership in a crisis at work or school or in the lives of friends who do not yet know God, offering you an opportunity to testify to your faith in Christ?

DAY 5

Pray: Ask God to speak to you through His Word, the Bible.

We arrive at the end of our journey as Paul ends his journey and arrives in Rome.

Luke has provided an account of the spread of the gospel and the increase of disciples and churches, starting in Jerusalem among believing Jews and going to the ends of the earth, to include all the nations. He ends the book with the longest summary statement in Acts, ending the final chapter:

> "Therefore let it be known to you that this salvation of God has been sent to the Gentiles; they will listen." He lived [in Rome] two whole years at his own expense, and welcomed all who came to him, proclaiming the kingdom of God and teaching about the Lord Jesus Christ with all boldness and without hindrance. (Acts 28:28-31)

Read: Acts 28

Reflect: Think back over this forty-day journey through Acts. Reflect on what you have learned as you read and reflected and what experienced as you applied this book to you life. To jog your memory, consider some of the following themes:

- *The story of God and the mission of the church*
- *The empowerment of the Holy Spirit for witness*
- *Being on mission and bold for Christ in your everyday life*
- *The importance of Christian community for discipleship and witness*
- *The role of persecution, suffering, and hardship on the path of discipleship and mission*
- *The role of personal and corporate prayer while we are on mission*
- *The power of the Spirit to radically transform lives*
- *Divine appointments in everyday life*

The story of Acts and the mission to witness to the whole earth until Christ returns is unfinished. You are part of the story. May God bless you and work mightily through you as you follow the Spirit's lead each day, live out God's kingdom priorities, and continue to live on mission with Jesus every day of your life.

APPENDIX

An Overview of the Story of God

ACT 1: THE OLD TESTAMENT

Scene 1: Creation

Creation

Scene 2: Separation

Scene 3: Promise

Scene 4: Sacrifice

Scene 5: Law

Scene 6: Kings

Scene 7: Prophets

Intermission: Four Hundred Years of Silence

Act 2: The New Testament

Scene 1: Salvation

Scene 2: Spirit

Scene 3: New Creation

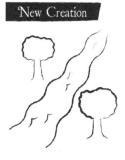

NOTES

1. A prerequisite of sorts for this guided journey through Acts is my book *The Story of God: A 40-Day Guided Journey through the Bible* or a basic knowledge of how the entire Bible story fits together. If you are confused about how the Bible fits together, I recommend starting with *The Story of God* or a similar study before venturing on this journey through Acts. If you decide to start here, I hope it whets your appetite to complete *The Story of God* journey after concluding this one.

ABOUT THE AUTHOR

H. Henry Williams is senior pastor at Five Oaks Church in Woodbury, Minnesota, where he has served since 1997. He is a graduate of Northwestern University in Saint Paul, Minnesota, Gordon-Conwell Theological Seminary, and Boston University (Doctor of Ministry). He served as an associate pastor for eight years at Westlink Christian Church (now Pathway Church) in Wichita, Kansas, and he served for five years on the faculty of The Center for Ministerial Education (an extension of Gordon-Conwell Theological seminary in urban Boston).

Henry is the author of *The Story of God: A 40-Day Guided Journey through the Bible*, available through Amazon.

For additional *Story of God* resources for churches and small groups, email Henry at hwilliams@fiveoakschurch.org

Follow Henry's blog at www.henry-williams.net.
Subscribe via email.

Follow Henry on Twitter: @HenryWilliams

30578720R00087

Made in the USA
Middletown, DE
29 March 2016